Short Lessons
in
Divine Science

By

NONA L. BROOKS

**CO-FOUNDER OF THE DIVINE SCIENCE COLLEGE
DENVER, COLORADO**

CONTENTS

———

Chapter		Pages
I	What Is the Fundamental Teaching of Divine Science?	5- 8
II	How Shall We Apply the Truth of Omnipresence to Our Daily Problems	9-13
III	What Is the Religion of Divine Science?	14-16
IV	Where Is God?	17-23
V	Why Are We Here?	24-28
VI	Why Should We Be Watchful of Our Thinking?	29-32
VII	How Shall We Pray?	33-35
VIII	How Shall We Solve Our Problems?	36-40
IX	How Shall We Keep Well?	41-43
X	What Is the Best Method of Healing?	44-48
XI	What Is Thought Training?	49-58
XII	How Can We Live In Harmony with Our Fellow Beings?	59-63
XIII	Can I Change My Disposition?	64-66
XIV	What Is Our Heredity?	67-70
XV	What Is the Greatest Human Achievement?	71-74
XVI	What Is Real and What Is Illusion?	75-83
XVII	When Shall We Realize Our Good?	84-90

A FOREWORD

All persons are more or less familiar with the fine work that is being done in natural science. We admire those who have so devotedly consecrated themselves to the discovery of the laws embodied in the natural world; we give them deep appreciation. During the past few years, however, there has come into the world something bigger and better even than natural science; something that includes the truth of natural science and leads the student to conclusions far more vital to his welfare than have ever before been given. Divine Science deals not merely with forms and forces, but goes back of these to the One Power that is responsible for the whole.

Students of Divine Science rejoice in the all-inclusiveness of this teaching. Nothing is excluded; all is to be understood and interpreted aright. An Omnipresent God does not confine the revelation of Himself to any one channel, but He flows into expression wherever He is given the right of way. Therefore every ardent and persistent seeker discovers Truth, and as a result contributes something toward the well being of mankind.

Again, we rejoice as we press further into the knowledge of this inexhaustible Truth that we find so much unity in all of the different lines of thought. The philosophies, the psychologies, the religions of the world become vibrant with life as we realize that these are revealing to us man's search for God—Truth. And what is more joy - bringing during this study than the certainty given that Knowledge of Truth means freedom for the individual? Freedom—no more bondage to the human limitations of sin, sickness and death, but a release into the Christ Consciousness, the liberty of the Sons of God.

This book of Short Lessons gives the steps that lead along the way from slavery to Sonship; from sickness to Health; from weakness to Power; from failure to Highest Success. It is to be studied slowly and thoughtfully. May it bless many in its journey into the world.

Let me here express my gratitude to Dr. Alice Ritchie and to Miss Miriam Mitchell for their interest in the little book and for the many helpful suggestions given me by them.

The Author.

I

WHAT IS THE FUNDAMENTAL TEACHING OF DIVINE SCIENCE?

Purpose: To give the student a simple and definite statement of the Principle upon which all Divine Science reasoning and every conclusion is based.

This lesson deals with Omnipresence, our basic teaching in Divine Science, and gives our reasons for believing in this Supreme Truth of the Universe. Divine Science lays its greatest emphasis upon Omnipresence. It is vital that the student should have this fundamental truth thoroughly grounded in thought before he proceeds to consider the further unfoldment of this system of teaching.

Knowledge of Omnipresence is necessary if one is to realize his God-given power.

Omnipresence! I hope that you will get a great deal of meaning out of this word, and that you will come to love it as I do. Moreover, I hope that what it suggests will come to be the very Guiding Power of your life.

Omnipresence! The many in the One and the One in the many; the All-Knowing, All-Powerful One.

All forms and forces are the expressions of Omnipresent, Intelligent Substance. There is just one Creator.

He who is religiously inclined, clothes this Supreme Truth in religious phraseology, and speaks of the All-Inclusive One as God. The scientifically inclined thinker will speak of the Infinite and Eternal Energy, the Cosmic Intelligence, from which all things proceed; while the philosopher will delight in the transcendent and immanent One.

Be certain that the idea—there is One and only One in all the universe—is clear to you, whatever form in language the thought my take.

"All are but parts of one stupendous whole, Whose body nature is, and God the Soul."

Spirit, Living Substance, God, is everywhere, and there is no other substance. Mind, the Infinite Intelligence of God, is everywhere, and there is no other intelligence.

Hence, we live in a Universe of God-Substance and God-Thought. To one who sees this, there comes the fulfilment of the prophecy of the new heaven and the new earth.

Divine Science did not accept lightly its doctrine of Omnipresence; and the years of teaching and demonstrating this Principle have proved its certainty.

Here are some of the reasons that have led us to accept Omnipresence as Truth:

The great spiritual seers of every age have believed it.

The Bible gives the same thought in many different ways.

Poets have sung it, and philosophers have used it as the basis of their philosophical systems.

Nature in her infinite variety of expressions proves Omnipresent Intelligence and Activity.

Jesus teaches it at every point.

It is interesting to see that even the natural scientists have discovered the same truth, and while some of them might reject the thought, when given in terms other than their own, nevertheless they are expressing the same idea very definitely. They affirm one substance in place of the many once proclaimed; they find one intelligence working everywhere, with one purpose, to one end. Therefore, unity has become a principle of natural science.

Again, the concept of Omnipresence is satisfying to the one who goes back of externals, and grasps the reality of things. It gives a principle of interpretation. It opens up new fields of research. It is a continuous delight mentally and spiritually.

When we accept Omnipresence as a working hypothesis; that is, when we assume Omnipresence to be Truth and live as if it were Truth, we find that our Principle works. It is applicable to all of our experiences and problems. We find healing, happiness, power, and success for ourselves and others, through the application of this Truth, that is, through the practice of the Presence of God.

The highest reason for the acceptance of Omnipresence is that when one has truly laid hold of the God-Consciousness, he *knows* that the One Presence is All.

First, then, in the attainment of power is the acceptance of this Basis, the Omnipresence, as the Truth of the Universe.

Or, if we cannot do this honestly, let us assume it as a working basis, in order that we may have the opportunity of proving for ourselves its truth. We who accept fully shall get easier and quicker results. We who assume this hypothesis shall, in time, discover for ourselves. We shall grow and shall finally be assured.

The reader is urged to make the contents of this chapter his own through study and practice, that he may be prepared to understand the next and to get full benefit from it. The following suggestions are given for daily practice for a week.

Think on the great Truth of Omnipresence in some such way as this—

Omnipresence is Truth.

This means that:

God includes me now.

God-Love is caring for me now.

God-Wisdom is guiding me now, in this problem.

God-Abundance is supplying my present need.

I can trust this Power and must not fear.

I am thankful for the Truth that makes me free.

These affirmations may be applied to others whom you wish to help.

Live faithfully by these truths, and you will find yourself unfolding into the realization of Power.

II

HOW SHALL WE APPLY THE TRUTH OF OMNIPRESENCE TO OUR DAILY PROBLEMS?

Purpose: To show that, through the application of Truth to the experiences of the day, each one of us may banish sickness and all inharmony.

This little book is for students, and it is taken for granted that you who are reading this lesson now have been faithful in your study and practice of Omnipresence, and that consequently you have realized the blessedness of a fuller understanding of its Truth.

Now, the questions come: "How can I make this Truth practical in my own life?" "How can I apply it more definitely to the experiences of the day?" "How can I use it in helping others to freedom from sickness and inharmony of every kind?"

The following suggestions are helpful:

Let us think of Omnipresence as Mind—the Wisdom, Knowledge, and Understanding of the Universal One, which evidences Itself as intelligence in the forms and forces of nature. In this understanding our affirmations will be:

Omnipresence is Mind, the Wisdom, Knowledge, and Understanding of the Universe.

Mind is here.

Mind includes me.

The province of Mind is to think.

The Universal Mind thinks according to Its Wisdom, Knowledge, and Understanding.

Thought, the activity of Mind, is the Creative Power of the Universe.

All things (forms) are thoughts of God.

The Law of the Universe is—Like begets like; thought is like the thinker.

God-Thought is Godlike; hence, God pronounces His Creation Good.

Universal Intelligence—God Mind active everywhere—Substance in manifestation—is Form, Man, the Individual.

Like begets like—the Individual is Godlike.

The Individual is begotten of God-Substance, Spirit; is formed by God-Intelligence; is partaker of God-Nature, Goodness.

This is the true state of Man.

All Substance is God-Substance; hence all Substance is perfect.

Substance does not change its nature by taking form.

Man, begotten of the Father, the Perfect Source, is perfect.

Each man can say, "My true state is perfection."

Study the foregoing until it is yours.

Now let us apply this Principle to the problems of the day.

In sickness what should we do?

Sit quietly and alone. Think for a few moments: God is here. Read thoughtfully the preceding affirmations. When our thought, through this method, has been fully withdrawn from externals, let us repeat several times: "God is Love; God is Peace." There comes a wonderful sense of the Presence; a great joy fills us because we are certain, very certain, of God and of God's Goodness.

While the blessedness of this realization is upon us let us turn our thought in deep love to the one whom we wish to help. We must forget the claim of sickness, or weakness, that is being made for him and by him, and know only the Truth. It helps sometimes to think directly to the person: "You are God's child; God's love surrounds you and cares for you; God's Power strengthens and sustains you; God's Life is yours. In the light of the Great Reality I see you perfect, free from the delusion of sin, sickness, death. I see you whole with God's Wholeness; I rejoice to speak this word for you; it is the Father that speaketh in me. The word of God is powerful to bless."

Never stop treating until you have made yourself certain of the truth, and with this certainty comes a feeling of rest; personal responsibility slips away as the assurance of God, the Living Factor in our lives, comes.

However, do not think that you have done your full part with this treatment. There is more help that you can give, and that is to take with you into the activities of the day this faith that you have realized in your time of meditation. Do not give credence to human opinion in regard to your patient.

Have faith in God's Presence as the Reality that is greater than climate, food, so-called material conditions, or human conceptions.

Again, if you wish to bring about concord between two persons where inharmony has seemed to prevail, the method would be the same. The thought emphasized should be that they both partake of the One Nature, Love, and that "Love is the Divine Adjuster."

If you wish to realize supply, withdraw thought from the contemplation of lack and its accompanying inconveniences, and give full attention to ever present abundance.

For fuller explanation and for help toward the realization of this abundance, which is now yours, I urge you to study our other publications and our text-book.

Live as if you believed in abundance; pay every debt, no matter how great the sacrifice; be true in every business transaction; be generous in attitude.

Rejoice in your good.

Demonstration is money in hand. Do not spend ahead of your realization, but get the *realization of plenty*. God is Abundance, and the Father has said, "All mine is thine."

What is the conclusion of the whole matter? What is the psychology of Divine Science? That we live in a Universe of Mind whose activity is Thought or Life.

That there is but One Mind. That we are dealing with One Mind, not many minds.

That all of our functions have a spiritual import. That we think and act in and by the One Mind. Hence, Life abounds in the richness of Universal Thinking. The truth of life is the truth of the Individual, Life's expression. Each man can say, "I live in Universal Wisdom, Knowledge, Undertanding. This realization frees me from every limitation placed upon me by my misconceptions or those of the race.

"God is my Father; I have no human heritage of thinking or of doing.

"God is my environment; I know no other presence.

"Love is my nature; I acknowledge no opposite.

"In God I am complete."

III

WHAT IS THE RELIGION OF DIVINE SCIENCE?

Purpose: To stimulate the student in his realization that the all important thing in his life is Love to God and to his fellow men.

It is necessary to know fundamental truth in order to live a well-directed life. This basic truth, Omnipresence, has been considered in the two preceding chapters. It is necessary to know the method of attainment, and this was given in the preceding lesson. However, there is still something that is necessary. We may understand both the philosophy and the psychology of Divine Science, and yet, if this be held as purely intellectual knowledge, it is not satisfying; we long for something more. Faithful practice of the principles given in these two phases of Divine Science brings to us the realization of the third phase, which is Love, the religion of Divine Science.

Religion, the realization of Love, brings richness, beauty, joy; it is true and abiding companionship with all there is; it gives us ability to serve with power, as well as to meet every human need, every soul hunger.

We usually interpret Love as conscious unity. Another satisfying interpretation is, "Love is out-streaming good-will." We may think about God and our fellow men in just the right way, without realizing this out-streaming good-will which is the essential in every relationship. Such a man will be called good, just, and upright, a man of *fine* character; but he has missed the very essence of life, *the feeling of oneness,* of companionship with God, and the joy of cooperation, of companionship with his fellow men. This man cannot evidence power in what he does; nor does he call forth love from others. A person of this sort is good but he is lonely. He has missed the secret of companionship and power.

An understanding of the principles of life is necessary; it is also essential to practice these in right thinking and right living; but it is religion, the realization of love, the warmth which glows through every experience, that truly blesses and uplifts.

If one is trying to progress without learning the meaning of God-Love, he is trying to tread the path without the light of day. If one is trying to preach, teach, or heal, without embodying in his thinking and living the never-failing Power, Divine Love, he is but sounding brass or a tinkling cymbal.

Love is the supreme gift; it is the kingdom of God within us.

"God is Love, and he who dwells in Love, dwells in God, and God in him."

Jesus gives two commandments: Thou shalt love the Lord thy God with all thy heart, and with all thy soul and with all thy mind. Thou shalt love thy neighbor *as thyself.* Paul sees that "Love is the fulfilling of the law"; that, above prophecy, above the understanding of mysteries, above knowledge, faith, and deeds of charity, is Love. To John who loved most was given wonderful visions of Truth.

Love is the only way to realize Truth, Life, Self, All. A pure fervent love for God is followed by love for all.

> Not love for one alone,
> But man as man thy brother own.
> —*Goethe.*

Let us practice love in our thinking and in our doing.

Is there a dreaded task ahead? Let us delight in service.

Is there suffering? Let us know that Divine Love is the healing Presence.

Is there limitation in any way? Let us know that God is abundance and that God is Love; Love shares its abundance with all .

Do you know anyone who is fearing or disliking another? Know that there is blessing and perfect forgiveness.

IV

WHERE IS GOD?

Purpose: *To make God's universality and His immediacy still more vivid to the student, and to show that Truth, wherever found, is One.*

All flesh shall come to worship before me, saith the Lord.—Isaiah 66:23.

And they shall not teach every man his neighbor and every man his brother, saying, Know the Lord: for all shall know me, from the least to the greatest.—Hebrews 8:11.

Schiller says, "There are three words that I would write in tracings of eternal light upon the hearts of men." And these three words are faith, hope, and love; the same that Paul chose for his wonderful discourse.

There is one word that I would write upon the hearts of men—Omnipresence.

Omnipresence! Repeat it to yourself; say it often; get the fullness of its meaning. It can never grow old; it will never become threadbare; it can never wear out. I prefer it to faith, hope, and love, because it is greater than these. Omnipresence is beyond hope; it is fulfilment. It is greater than either faith or love, because it includes these, and more within itself. Omnipresence, the All-Presence, the Presence that is always present!

This Presence is around us right now, and It is in us; It is around, through, and in all; It fills heaven and earth.

The Presence dwells everywhere even to the uttermost parts of the Universe, now and forever.

What is our name for Omnipresence—"The Presence that filleth all"? We love to speak of it as God, the Father, Infinite Mind, Source and Cause, Principle. It, in fact, makes but little difference what name we use; the vital matter is that we understand this Presence, and live in the consciousness of It.

A gentlemen came in one day to ask, "What is Divine Science?" I had talked with him only a few moments, when he said, "I see that you base your teachings on God and the Bible. Now, friend, I wish to say in all kindness that you will never have a live religion as long as you cling to those fossilized ideas."

Then he proceeded to give his own idea of the eternal realities. He told me that there were two things that I must bear in mind in order to understand him. First, that he never soared away into infinity as most people did when talking religion; he never went above the tree-tops. And, secondly, that he was a materialist. "You say all is spirit; I say all is matter." Rather uncompromising at first glance, wasn't it? The remainder of his creed was interesting. He carried matter back to the most subtle form conceivable, back to the atom, back of the theory of ether. This rarefied matter was everywhere, and from it and within it all action, all creation takes place. His name for this omnipresence was atomic energy. I said, "May I ask you a few questions to be sure that I understand you?" My request was granted.

"This atomic energy is everywhere?"

"Yes."

"It makes everything?"

"Yes."

"It works methodically, according to law and order, and knows what is going to be the result of its action?"

"Yes."

"It knows its own nature, that it is omnipresent, that it can do all things, and how all things are done?"

"Certainly."

"What it makes is like itself; that is, the same substance and nature?"

"Yes."

"Then," I said, "we are much nearer together than you think; we have the same idea of Omnipresence; you call it atomic energy, we call it God. We have the same idea of substance; you call it matter; we call it Spirit. We vary in terms, but not in the idea that these terms represent. This is the essential unity."

There are times when it seems necessary to set forth the difference between what we believe and what others believe. When this is necessary, we do it fearlessly, but always in love. However, I see clearly that the oneness of faith we so much desire will never be brought about by our emphasizing this difference, but rather by a constant recognition of that in which we agree. I love to dwell on points of similarity and unity; I love to feel my oneness with others. Next to this joy is that of knowing that they, too, are conscious of the existence of this unity.

No matter how much we may differ in minor points, if we stand together in the consciousness of Omnipresence, not only is our basis one, but our motives, our aims, our accomplishments are also one. The only difference is in the method employed to carry out our purpose.

The realization of Omnipresence! Please go back of the word, every time I use it; go in thought to Omnipresence Itself.

The realization of the Presence will bring to us wonderful consciousness not only of our oneness with God but of our unity with all mankind.

This is the foundation of all the good that we may do our fellow men, of all the help we can give them. We can not go into the slums of our large cities with the manner of superior beings sent from a different sphere to a peculiar people, and lead them away from vice and filth to their own true selves. On the other hand, we, who through consciousness of Omnipresence, come into a true understanding of brotherhood, can extend our hands to these needy ones as man to man, brother to brother, and lead them out of every condition into the understanding of God as a loving Father and of men as one with Him and one with each other. Herein lies the salvation of the world, and the only salvation there is, for this is Truth, the Christ-Principle.

Omnipresence teaches us that in the depths of each man's heart, no matter how frivolous he may be, or how material and degraded he may seem, there is a consciousness of God;

Feeble, perhaps, in some; but it is there. This consciousness longs to spread itself, to grow until it takes entire possession of the individual. You and I knowing this, may speak to this great consciousness, not always with the lips, but with the heart, always. Let us recognize its presence, and encourage its progress by this steadfast recognition, until we find ourselves in heart to heart comradeship with those we touch in the day's work. In this way alone can we stand side by side with them, and help them to realize their ideal of the purer, truer life; for the ideal is there within each one and it may be realized.

The noblest, the most sacred, the happiest mission in life is to help our fellow men to a higher realization. The privilege of helping is ours. Realization of Omnipresence brings us into closer relation with our fellow men; it introduces into our daily lives that element of love whose warmth and brightness is much needed here.

It brings us into relationship with all that men have believed the world over, for as we take a greater interest in mankind, we desire to know men better, and we are interested in their views on vital subjects. Our desire is to know how much of Truth has been revealed to men, and how much of Omnipresence they have realized. This desire leads us to pay attention to the different faiths presented to the world; and we are glad to find, as we always shall, if we investigate, that there is not so much difference in the teachings of the various religions as we had imagined. For if we are willing to go back of the form of worship, back of the word to the heart of each, no matter how material it may seem at first, we shall find Omnipresence declaring Itself even there.

The following quotations from Ebers give, he says, a brief summary of what have been found to be some of the secret teachings of the Egyptian priesthood, kept secret because they thought that they could disclose these to the favored few only, who on account of special virtue or wisdom, were ready to comprehend them.

"We know that the Godhead is one; we name it 'The All,' 'The Veil of the All,' or simply Ra; but under the name, Ra, we understand something different from that which is known to the common herd; for to us the universe is God and, in each of its parts, we recognize a manifestation of that highest Being without whom nothing is, in the heights above or in the depths below.****

"Whether we view the sun, the harvest, or the Nile, whether we contemplate with admiration the harmony or unity of the visible or the invisible world, still it is always with the only, the all-embracing One that we have to do, to whom we also ourselves belong as those of His manifestations in which he places His self-consciousness."

Again we read, "All that He—the One—has created is penetrated with His own essence and bears witness to His goodness. He who knows how to find Him, sees Him everywhere, and lives at every instant in the enjoyment of His glory."

I quote this simply as an illustration of what I have just said about finding the unity in all religions. Even in this form of worship, outwardly so idolatrous, when we get back of the outward form, we find our own perception of God's Presence and Power.

Our oneness with God, with our fellow man and with the Truth as it is found in all religions is a result of a realization of Omnipresence.

There is still something more that Omnipresence reveals to us—our oneness with the entire creation. When we understand this, it is very precious to us; for man is restored to his rightful position of unity with, instead of subjection to, the visible. When we look upon the mountains, the plains, the flowers, the trees, and the animal world, let us say within ourselves, "The same Power that formed my body formed them; the same Presence that dwells in me, is in them." We are one, for are we not the same in origin, in substance, and in life? Then, indeed, shall we find "sermons in stones, books in running brooks, and good in everything." With this understanding comes the realization of our true dominion, and of our perfect freedom from so-called physical law.

Our realization of Omnipresence does not make it true, but because it is true we may realize it; and this realization will broaden our individuality to the length, breadth, height, and depth of the Universe. There is but one thing that Omnipresence does not include and that is —What shall I call it? Ignorance, false beliefs, darkness, sin. Call it what you will.

That which is opposed to God—of an opposite nature—has no place in Omnipresence for, broad as it is, there is room for but one, and that one is God.

"I am God, and there is none else."—Isa. 45: 22.

V

WHY ARE WE HERE?

Purpose: *To show man's part in his own salvation.*

Individual life is for the purpose of unfoldment; progress is the watchword. In the highest conception it is self-expression. There are two stages in individual development. Of one, Paul speaks: "The heir, so long as he is a child, differeth nothing from a servant, though he be lord of all." While the individual is thinking of himself as a slave to everything, and carrying out this belief by existing in a condition of bondage or limitation, he is, all of the time, "lord of all," but he does not know it. He is developing toward the realization.

There is the childhood and the manhood of the individual. When he is a child in understanding, he has no knowledge of his true nature or of his power. He is ignorant and innocent; but the power of Love is caring for the individual, and he is compelled to develop. In the childhood of the individual, there is always the seeking of happiness, of what the child calls good. Though he may make many errors, this desire is really his prayer, and it is answered by infinite Love in the way that is best for his unfoldment. The Spirit of Wisdom and Love knows better than the one who desires and prays ignorantly. This childhood is a stage of trouble. It takes life as a burden, because of its ignorance.

Manhood comes when the individual knows the Truth of his being or of his eternal and changeless state. When he knows his power, he enters his kingdom, and realizes that he is lord of all.

We are now in tne transition period, dropping things of childhood, and realizing some of the things of manhood. Childhood is subject to limitation; it separates itself from God and man. Manhood begins to unite, to recognize Universal Presence and Power. Man is touching the hem of the garment of Truth. There is much more to know and greater power to realize. We find the development into manhood, a freeing process; life, instead of slavery, gives mastery. Many are living in the period of childhood; others are passing into manhood. The undeveloped condition breeds poverty, sickness, and death. Happiness therein depends upon the outer, therefore men work hard to bring to themselves money, friends, things—whatever they consider desirable. We shall never get anything from the outer but what we take to it. The thing we meet on every hand is first found within our mentality. Always striving for outer benefits, we are still unhappy, until we find the kingdom within.

Man must redeem his own life. By his mistakes has his conception of life become distorted. By rectifying these mistakes shall his distorted views of life be changed, and his redemption accomplished. Simple living is to be desired above all else.

There is nothing grander than genuine simplicity; nothing that will so cause us to stand out as strong

men and women. **The first step toward living simply is directness.**

This means that the individual must make his own connection with God, the universal Life. Man must gain spiritual knowledge for himself. "Religion is the life of God in the soul of man."

Direct living establishes our connection with God.

The realization of this close communion is the purpose of every silence, the outcome of every treatment. When it is attained we can say, "I and my Father are one." Imagine the power in understanding life from this conscious unity with the Perfect Life.

Man must act directly from the Center of Life within.

This enables one to live what may be called the spontaneous life. Consciousness of life thus gained must go forth expressing as directly as it has received. Such consciousness is not borne in upon by what people are saying; it is not bound by old conventions, but is living from its own center, is thinking and speaking freely and fully, and is beginning to make us lifters rather than leaners.

Our Science stands for law and order. Not to be limited by conventionality does not mean to be lawless. "To thine own self be true, and it must follow as the night the day, thou canst not then be false to any man."

The direct life does not live on the surface, but goes to the root of things. It connects with the great Central Energy of the Universe, and there is no waste of power or energy in its work.

This directness gives consciousness of power; it ensures a life of peace; it takes away fear. A life of freedom is the fruit of the simple life that comes forth spontaneously as a result of living directly from our inmost Center. Jesus' life was the simplest we can think of. We cannot imagine that he could ever have done anything for the sake of show, or that he refrained from anything for fear of what people would say. Show impresses children; they of fuller understanding appreciate simplicity. Great men are not afraid to act naturally; that is, according to their nature. This does not mean to act unkindly or selfishly, if we feel so. When living in and from that Center within, we shall not hold such feeling; sensitiveness falls away.

Until the true Center of action is found and our consciousness is made alive to our union with that Center within, we act according to conventionalities, and are bound by unnatural laws to man-made limitations.

Thought training will help us to abide in our center. If I feel anger, let me stop and think; let me not speak that feeling, but the opposite. Love spoken will soon destroy every feeling of anger. "A soft answer turneth away wrath."

Live from within, if you would have power and peace.

Manhood is the goal. We do not ask a child learning to walk to carry a chair across a room. We learn to place each one where he belongs. Keep in thought the ideal man, the perfection of man.

In knowledge of perfection we go forth not to resist or to conquer, but by co-operation, to express.

Such a one knows that he has no trouble either in mental attitude or in outer conditions. The Inner and the outer are full of Divine Life and Love. Love means conscious unity. One who loves knows himself at one with all that is.

Each of us can say, "All power in the universe has been given unto me. .

"Universal Power is expressing through me, to me, and for me. All that is, is for me. The universe is working for me." All nature is on the side of the man that tries to rise. Each of us is wonderfully precious in God's sight, and the whole universe is not too much for a child of God.

VI

WHY SHOULD WE BE WATCHFUL OF OUR THINKING?

Purpose: To show the importance of right thinking.

We lay great stress on right thinking, because from thinking come results in our lives, words and deeds.

If thought is right, we shall speak truly and do our best. Character arises from habit of thought. A man of strong, positive thought will be a man of strong character. Habit of thought is an indication of character. We cannot think loving thoughts and be unkind. Health depends upon our thinking. Environment is also affected by our thinking. If our environment is not such as belongs to one who thinks right thoughts, let us change our thinking.

To change environment or outer conditions we do not have to work directly with them but with our own thinking about them.

If we think rightly, we shall change either our mental attitude toward environment, or environment itself — whichever needs changing. Our accomplishment in every direction, all that we do in the world, in business and in domestic life, is affected by our mental attitude. Hence it is worth while to cultivate right habits of thinking.

Every thought writes something. The true thought is recorded faithfully and the untrue thought, with equal certainty.

Every thought, whether spoken or not, brings about a result.

We once believed that it mattered but little how often we grew angry within, if this anger was not expressed, and that we could think ill of one provided that we did not voice the sentiment. Now we know that thought is always recorded outwardly; if not in speech, in other ways. I have often wondered what the effect would be if thought appeared in visible form before us—the good thought as a form, good to see, and the ill thought as an ill-fashioned form. Do you not think that we would then be more careful of our thinking?

All inharmony is the result of our letting ourselves think that which is opposite to truth.

Every object has come forth from Mind Universal. Even the house we live in, the clothes we wear, the paintings we admire, were all thought out, then wrought out; the Intelligence that thought these out is Divine, God thinking through man; the Power that wrought these out is God-Power working through man. The world about us is a constant evidence of God's living thought for us.

Everything rests first in Mind. To know and to grasp this is to lay hold of a wonderful principle.

Thought is based upon perception. To a limited view life is narrow. To a broad full perception, life is deep and rich. Perfect thinking depends upon perfect knowledge. The process by which we learn to think aright is that by which we go below the surface of things and view the situation from this standpoint. He who goes below the surface has insight. Insight reveals the truth of things, and from this the world takes on a new hue. Things that we once resisted, we now feel kindly towards. Instead of struggling to attain, we gain insight into the principle of attainment. We believe the primary truths of Being, and thought born of such understanding expresses the best without struggle.

The first step toward knowing the truth of things is to seek the truth earnestly.

No matter what we have believed, we must be willing to reverse it, if truth reveals a newer version. Truth is ever going to unfold to us more and more, if we hold ourselves receptive. Never stand still and say that there is nothing more. Truth is ever revealing to us that receptivity is the open door through which we shall realize more and more fully the powers of the Universal Life. When we say, "I can go no farther," we shut ourselves off from that unfoldment. After the perception of fundamental principles what are we to do? We must certainly do more than accept. After perception and acceptance, thought is to be trained in the Truth every day.

We have not seen life truly; hence we have believed in two powers, two substances. The study of Truth teaches us better. This is perception. We lay hold of its meaning, and then think. First, perception comes; then thought-training follows until consciousness becomes clear. After this no more thought training, for right thinking is spontaneous. It comes because we are conscious of Truth, and we enter heaven. We are conscious of our divinity, and we live out this Divinity.

Systematic right thinking solves every problem in our daily lives.

Right thinking leads to the realization that the successful life is the life that meets the purpose for which it is here, and that this purpose is attainment, unfoldment, the development of the individual—the making of a Man. Every experience, condition, and circumstance, that comes to us is for the purpose of our development, and will be helpful according to the spirit in which we meet it, and the wisdom with which we handle it.

Growth is attained through Self-expression.

Self-expression is induced by every demand made upon one, by every hardship, by every so-called obstacle that he meets. The strong man has always had what is called a hard life; how else could he become conscious of strength? How else could he prove his strength?

True thinking shows us the meaning of what we are calling difficulties: they are opportunities for the development of the individual, not hindrances.

"The strong man rejoices to run the race." If we are to measure the success of life, we must read the soul aright. Here and here alone is the true, and indelible, and infallible witness of all achievements. Here we find the only result worth looking for.

VII

HOW SHALL WE PRAY?

Purpose: To show why we pray and the best method of prayer.

A new conception of God calls for a new method of prayer. We no longer feel that we must overcome God's reluctance, but rather that we are to lay hold of His willingness. More willing is He to give than we are to receive. In order, then, to learn how to pray, let us turn to our Basis, Omnipresence. This means God everywhere; therefore God includes me. I can say with authority, "I am in God and God is in me. Therefore I share God-Being, God-Mind, God-Life." "All mine is thine, saith the Lord." By sharing Himself with us God gives us every good gift. Before we call, He has supplied. God is Abundance.

If I seem to lack any good thing it is because I have not believed fully in God's Immediate Presence.

God is doing His part. I do not need to beg or to ask Him to do more. But I must do my part.

I must train my thought to recognize steadfastly the immediacy and fullness of God's Presence.

I must not permit an opposing thought to stay. What is the commonest opposing thought? It is fear; for fear denies the presence of God. Hence we must not permit fear thought to stay for a moment. We can put it out by denying it, and also by substituting for fear its opposite, conscious unity, love; by affirming, "I do not fear, for God is here this moment," and by repeating this statement with positiveness until all fear goes.

Inharmony of any kind, sickness or lack, shows that we are ignoring God's presence.

Let us affirm that which is consistent with God-Presence: health, ever-present, changeless health; supply, ever-present, abundant supply.

But this is not all of prayer; in fact, it is the lesser part. Prayer is active communion. There is no passivity or resignation in prayer. When we have prayed, let us answer our own prayer. God has answered it before we called. Let us affirm the presence of All-Good. Our affirmations are for the purpose of clearing our mentality of wrong conceptions and of establishing within it the certainty of God—health, abundance, power, joy.

We bring our own prayers to fulfillment by living them out in our lives.

Let me illustrate: An unhappy condition exists between me and a friend of long standing. It hurts. I learn by turning to my Basis that I can right it by prayer. I deny separation in God-Presence, and affirm, that as children of God, we share His Divine nature and are therefore loving and kind always. I make this prayer once a day or as often as opportunity offers. Now for the answering of this prayer within myself. I must watch my thinking between my prayers, that it keeps true to the prayer. I must let no thought of anger, fear, or hurt stay in my thinking. Perfect Love, which I have affirmed, and which is the Truth of God and of myself, casts out the opposites. I have prayed for perfect love. I must demonstrate it in thought and deed. This is the royal road to heaven—harmony of living.

After praying and living quietly the love prayed for, there usually comes an opportunity to serve the friend; to do something kind for him or her. I must do it with joy and without ostentation of self-consciousness. If the service meets with rebuff, I will not allow myself to be discomfited, but I will persist in my attitude of love, remembering that "Love endureth all things, thinketh no evil"—conquers every adverse condition.

True prayer which consists of right thinking and right living, never fails.

It corrects our mistakes, makes us healthful, happy, more loving and more efficient; it brings realization of Good along many lines. Praying does all of this by bringing to us a deeper and clearer realization of God-Presence. Through this realization we are uplifted, purified, glorified; we radiate God-Qualities. Our lives are answered prayers. Our word and our work go out into the world from the radiant Center of Truth, to uplift, to bless, to heal.

VIII

HOW SHALL WE SOLVE OUR PROBLEMS?

Purpose: To show that problems are not our enemies but our friends; that they are our opportunities to demonstrate. Also to give the three Principles to be demonstrated in solving them.

We are here to grow, and we grow by solving our problems. To solve a problem means to get the right answer. We are not to be resigned to hard conditions—our unsolved problems. We are to solve our problems; and they are to be solved with power. How shall we do this? First of all—

We must take the right attitude toward our environment with its multifold processes.

In order to bring ourselves to this attitude, we are to remember that:

The goal of all growth is the realization of God as the only Presence and Power.

Every one is on his way to his goal. Some are farther along than others.

Problems vary according to one's development.

A problem, when rightly met, becomes a stepping stone to greater unfoldment.

Many so-called problems, when understood, are no longer hardships but blessings.

Sometimes more or less quickly according to our faithfulness, we shall realize steadfastly our oneness with the Father. In this realization there are no problems.

The great discovery of the eighteenth century was that law included everything and controlled everything. The still more wonderful discovery of the twentieth century is that law extends also to the inner life of the individual. The mental, moral, and spiritual phases of our being are lawful. It is a marvelous experience for us to come to understand that we are subject to inharmony only as long as we submit to it. Enlightenment will free us. Jesus says, "Ye shall know the truth and the truth shall make you free."

As long as we believe that God sends suffering, we shall consider trouble and disease inevitable; but when we come to know the Truth of God's Omnipresence and are convinced that God is blessing us always with health and all good, we shall see that we do not have to be ill or inharmonious.

We shall accept our birthright of perfect harmony, physical, mental, and spiritual.

Every process, every experience is according to law. We are where we are in circumstance and in development by law, not by chance. As we come into the understanding of the great principles of the universe, and train ourselves to practice these in our thinking, we live powerfully, and problems disappear from our experience.

Strength is brought forth in solving problems. Latent force is evolved that we should otherwise not be conscious of possessing. A problem is a call upon us to come forth—to express what is within. It is an opportunity to learn more of principle, to lay hold of the depth of Being, and to prove its truth. Problems cease as problems; that is, the problematical part ceases, but not the opportunity to demonstrate what we know. A problem solved is no longer a problem.

There will always be the inner and the outer life, or Life-Principle and its visible manifestation. Principle never changes; outer events and incidents vary, and we also change our attitude toward them, thus putting a different interpretation upon them.

Life is not a struggle; it is only lack of conscious ness that makes the struggle in living.

Do not call your problems troubles; there is but one trouble in the world—our mental attitude toward things, the view we take of them. Face your troubles; ask the meaning; seek to know the purpose.

There are two ways by which we may get rid of trouble. We may change our mental attitude; we may see everything as opportunity. What once made us weep, will make us happy.

Inharmonies, whether mental or bodily, mean that we have stepped aside from the Path of Truth.

They are the warning voice that says, "Come back; get hold again; be positive." If we could wander from the consciousness of God's Presence and be comfortable, we might stay there; but troubles and sickness are the prods that push us back to realize nearness to God. They are continually saying, "Come up higher." Poverty says, "Bring forth your wisdom and strength. Apply your knowledge and understanding." As long as we are in the place of changing conditions we need spurs to action. We fill our lives with companionship, not by seeking but by giving. The new phase of life is non-resistance; not taking arms against a sea of trouble, but lifting our thoughts into clear perception. Everything is co-operating with us. We have failed to meet the demand, but the universe is forcing us to co-operate. There is no separation; all is unity. In this consciousness we can see that problems are opportunities.

The three supreme principles that we are to demonstrate in solving our problems are:

I. Unity—

All are expressions of One Whole. All are included in the One.

"There is one God and Father of all, who is above all, and through all, and in you all," is Paul's way of putting it. Jesus sees himself and us in the Father. Both Paul and Jesus demonstrated this principle when they gave themselves in loving service to humanity.

II. Goodness—

We partake of the nature of God.

To demonstrate this in powerful living, there must be perfect integrity in every relationship —in our domestic, social, and business activities.

III. Abundance—

Mankind, begotten of God, is included in the Life Universal, the Life that abounds in richness.

Each soul shares with all humanity in these Infinite Treasures.

When we take these principles as our working basis, and demonstrate them in our living, we find that one by one our problems are solved. A great peace comes to us. We rejoice in a new realization of Power. We shout from the depths of our being.

All things are possible to him who believes in God's Allness, God's Goodness, God's Abundance.

IX

HOW SHALL WE KEEP WELL?

Purpose: To show that health is natural; that it is the birthright of every person.

Health is natural; disease is abnormal.

When we come to know *Ourselves,* we shall live in such accord with the Laws of Being that our health will "spring forth speedily."

To learn the truth of Life, we must go to the Basis—Omnipresence. From this standpoint each one of us has a right to say, "I am born of God; I am included in God; I am inseparable from God." To know God aright is health, eternal health; for to know God aright is to know Self aright in God, of God, like God.

Man has never lost his Divine Nature; he is just discovering it.

To be endowed with Divine Nature is to be endowed with Divine Wholeness. Health therefore, is ours now. Since this is Truth, why are we ill? The question is easily answered. Through ignorance we have false concepts of life; we misinterpret, and live according to our misconceptions. These false views are in themselves inharmony, and conceal from us the great realities—Love, Peace, Joy, Health.

If we believe in many powers, some good, some evil, we fear the evil powers. This attitude of fear shapes all kinds of monsters in our thoughts. We tremble and cringe; slaves to our own imaginings. However, when we understand the Truth of God's Loving Presence and Infinite Power, our attitude changes; our thinking is illumined; the body is revealed to us as it really is, formed of Spirit-Substance, alive with Divine Life, cared for by Infinite Intelligence— perfect, harmonious, and free always. This realization is health.

Sometimes we perceive Truth and accept it fully, but we are so fixed in the old habit of thought, that realization of freedom does not come readily. How can this intellectual perception be changed to realization?

Realization is brought about by the steadfast practice of the Presence of God.

What is meant by practicing the Presence?

Suppose that I awaken in the morning with the dread of the day upon me. I lie for a moment hard pressed with the burden of work, monotony, or experience, that is ahead of me. Suddenly I remember my decision to practice the Presence. I think of this Presence as Love, the Love in which I live, move, and have my being; the Love that blesses me with strength and joy. I resolve to live by this, and rising quickly, I go joyfully to the day's activities because I am certain of this loving care. I put aside doubt and dread, and rejoice that I am given wisdom to meet every experience in strength. Or, perhaps, I have a tendency to despondency; then the word joy should be my practice for the day. I should repeat as I dress, and as I work, "Joy, joy, I am glad I am alive." If I remain true to this joyous attitude in every kind of experience, at night I find that this day has been easy, not hard; bright, not gloomy.

If I tend to irritability or quick temper, I must take love as my practice word, and be true to the thought of love until the old habit fades away. Or I may be thrown with those who hold the belief of illness; life, health, peace, would be helpful words. To these I speak silently, living words. "God's perfect Life is there within you, around you. It is active now for your good. Trust this intelligent Life. It is doing its perfect work." I must repeat this statement until the truth of it becomes apparent. I must refuse to see the opposite, the shadow side. I must stand true to Reality no matter what the appearance may be.

While I am training myself to live the Truth faithfully, I am growing daily in the Wisdom and Knowledge of God; I am practicing the Presence of health, and I am unfolding steadily into greater realization.

X

WHAT IS THE BEST METHOD OF HEALING?

Purpose: To present to the student briefly the three methods of metaphysical healing.

While healing in its largest sense includes many different lines of realization, the term usually means realizing health of body. It is, today, interesting to watch the amount of attention that is being given to healing in the newspapers, magazines, and churches. This is encouraging, because it is indicative of the present trend of thinking. There is on all sides an awakening toward higher thinking.

There are now few churches that spurn healing. The limitations of tradition are fading in the light of this new freedom that the world of men is feeling. The healing of the nations is coming through the healing of the heart. Is there a best way to bring this about? It seems so to me, and I think I have found it. There are three kinds of metaphysical healing.

The first is mental healing. The purpose of this method is to develop the mentality of the individual, the personal will, in order that it may overcome personal ills. Mental Science tells us that if we develop our will and are faithful, we shall have the power of suggestion to heal another. This method often brings outward harmony for a time but there are several mistakes here. The first is the exalting of the personal self, for if one does not remain very humble, he acquires the egotistical habit, and rides rough-shod over his fellow men, certain of the effect of strong will-power. Another difficulty is that an untrained mentality formulates without any basis for decision. We cannot trust the personal will; we can trust the Divine Will.

Perfection in every phase of life is God's Will for us.

The second type is faith healing. In this method God is besought until he answers. However, since we have come to know God as Omnipresent Life, Health, and Good, we no longer beseech Him for any gift, for we know that He has already given us all Good.

The purpose of prayer is not to change God but ourselves.

God does not need changing; He is ever present health. His will is that we shall know this and rejoice in perfect harmony of body, circumstance, and relationship.

This realization comes to us through the third type of healing. Divine Science, true to its basis, the Omnipresence of God, declares that an ever present God means unchanging health for each one of us, and this we realize by using scientific treatment. Scientific treatment has two phases: The silent time when one affirms God's Presence and denies what is unlike His Presence, until one feels the truth of what he is saying. Then one must go into the activities of the day with the consciousness of God's Presence, making each thought and act true, loving, and powerful. This is the highest method of healing and brings the richest and most lasting results within and without, for it reveals the Perfect Whole.

What do I mean by The Perfect Whole—Universal Presence? Think of the air. We are all breathing it no matter whether we live in darkest Africa or in America. Wherever our brother is on the face of the globe, we know that he is breathing the same air that we are. You see the analogy. Could there be any one who thinks that the same God is not manifesting in the very heart of darkest Africa? God is everywhere. Divine Science stands on the foundation of Omnipresence. Omnipresence is the blessed truth that we live, move, and have our Being in God, and that God acts by means of man. Infinite Being is the One Presence, the One Creator. All activity is the expression of this Power.

We can lay hold of the great law of the Cosmic Energy, and build true to it in our thinking and living.

From the bringing forth of a plant to the fitting of a joint in carpentry, there is evidence of One Creative Power and only One. This One brings forth without ceasing, and all that It brings forth is like Itself, very good. The image that It conceives is true to Principle. Since God, the Perfect One, is the only Creator, creation is Godlike. It is perfect, beautiful, whole. When we see God in Creation, we see that Creation is the perfect expression of Idea eternally unfolding as the visible world.

What is it, then, that makes us see inharmony? Emphasis laid on externals leads to misconception. We are seeing partially, hence imperfectly.

True seeing is healing. When we see the Truth of the Self, we are healed.

When we see rightly, the true creation of God is revealed. All inharmony disappears.

Well I remember my first experience of cosmic consciousness. I was sitting in a small, plainly furnished healing room in the first home of Divine Science in Denver. I see before me now the ordinary sofa and an equally commonplace chair. The walls are bare. In the work that had come that morning, I had realized God's Presence and Power to an unusual degree. Suddenly as I sat meditating, I saw that a brightness, a veritable glory was filling the room. The walls radiated light; the sofa had changed as well as the simple chairs. I was seeing the true life of this room. It was alive with the Presence. There was nothing old. All things had become new. I was seeing with the inner vision. This Presence is aliveness, and within it we know there is no ugliness, no inharmony.

Divine Science teaches infinite Power, and has as its highest realization, God, the Omnipotent Thinker, thinking forth creation.

In nature man is perfect—one with his Creator. Of myself I am nothing; I am all things in God. I claim for all men this same wholeness, completeness, and perfection.

What is the truth about healing? Leave the body with the Creator; in His sight it is perfect. Take a stand in the Omnipresence of health and power. Do not touch the body in thought: We do not have to recreate tissue or rebuild organs.

The secret of healing lies in directing thought toward the Creator, not toward the appearance.

We must work to change our mental outlook, not the body. Denials and affirmations are mental exercises. What shall we deny? Only the general things. For example say, "I will not admit this or that unreality to my thought. I deny fear. There is no fear. Human belief is tempting me to be afraid; but, 'Get thee behind me, Satan'."

Fear has no place in our Divine make-up.

If we allow it to do so, fear can keep us in hell. Hence deny any belief opposite to God as the only Creator. Do not let evil weaken your realization of the Presence and Power of God. Take hold of the world from the God-side. God is the life and the blessedness of His world.

What is the best method of healing? That which gives the most general and far-reaching results; that which is most permanent and most preventive. The test of a method of healing is, "How deep does it reach? Does it reach the center of a man's being?"

Healing must include the whole man—his body, his environment, his circumstances as well as his Spirit.

The only method that can do this is the one which sees man one with God—whole, complete, perfect. When we grasp this method, we find the preventive for all future disease and lack. We assert that monistic healing has the true basis, and that "All things are possible to them that believe." Truth never fails; it is only our grasp of Truth that fails. Let us keep our grasp steadfast and our vision clear.

XI

WHAT IS THOUGHT TRAINING?

*Purpose: To show how the intellectual per-
ception of our good may be changed into the
consciousness of already possessing that good.*

I have been giving the basis of healing in
order that each one might know why we believe
in healing, and how it may be done. There are
two things that I wish to recall to your attention,
because they are two important items, if we are
going to understand many things in the healing
work. First, there comes to us in our search for
Truth, the perception of Truth. We reason; we
listen; we decide that a certain thing, a certain
thought presented, is the Truth. If it is Truth,
it is something to be known positively and to be
lived. After this perception, we reach out; we
wish more. We have taken a good step, but we
are not perfectly satisfied, and never shall be,
until there comes to us something that is in-
describable; That Something we call consciousness. We perceive a great deal of Truth of
which we have not yet become conscious. What
is the link? How can we develop from the
perception into the consciousness of Truth?
Thought training is the link; thought is the
instrument of the work.

**After we have perceived Truth, the next thing for
us to do is to work in thought until we come to the
consciousness of Truth.**

**The three steps in the process of unfoldment then
are: first, perception, followed by thought training in
that perception, then consciousness—realization.**

When consciousness comes, we have reached the place of peace, the place of rest. The place of peace and rest is not the place of inactivity, because the place of the most powerful action is that which comes forth spontaneously from consciousness. When we are conscious, the effort to act, the effort to express is ended, and the expression of the Truth of which we are conscious, is free, joyful, spontaneous. Remember that most of us in our present place of unfoldment are working from perception to consciousness, and this is the reason that so much attention is given to the training of thought.

I have heard words like these: "I have been treating for months; I have been thinking this way for a long time, and yet I am not well. Conditions are not removed." The mere speaking of the word is not the whole; it is but a means to an end. The person who comes to you with such a statement, shows you that the Consciousness has not come to her or to him. It is but a mechanical process of which this person is speaking—good in its place, yes; but power, peace, and harmony will come to us only when we are conscious of Truth. Each of us is just as peaceful, just as harmonious and just as powerful, as he is conscious, not a bit more nor less.

Consciousness is the one thing to be worked for.

When I say, worked for, do not think that I mean any straining, any labored work. I mean a steadfast determination to gain the realization of Truth, and a peaceful, persistent going forward to the accomplishment—the attainment of consciousness. It will never be refused to anyone who is faithful, according to law, and law never changes. No one can ever hold us back. We alone retard our own development.

There is a great difference between curing and healing. We have much of both in our midst, and if we understand this, many problems are solved for us. Here are examples of the three methods previously discussed. A patient comes to a healer, and tells a lengthy tale of woe; the healer goes to work sending the thought directly to the body of the patient; thus the patient through suggestion comes under the domination of the healer's personal will, in order to build up tissue or to regulate action. While some cures are wrought by this method, it is through personal will power, and does not lead to the highest realization.

Again, there is the one who says, "All ills are mental. I will send my thoughts to the thought of the patient." Hence he begins using suggestion and the power of personal will. The healer endeavors to change the thought of the patient, and some good work is done in this way.

In the second method, which is known as faith healing, the worker attempts to turn the thought of his patient to prayer. He says, "Let us beseech the Father to heal you." But we know that God is not moved, for He is our health now. He knows only health—wholeness.

The third, the method that is best, as we see it, the one that we should seek above all things else, because it goes so much deeper, is this: Some one comes to the healer to ask for healing. What is the healer to do?

He is not to send out his thought to the body or to the mentality of the patient, but to turn his thought directly to God.

Turn there, and train thought to listen to what the Universal Spirit is saying. The Universal Spirit speaks of Life Omnipresent; It speaks of Love changeless; It tells of the infinite power of this Presence; thought listening there becomes illumined. There will be no more great effort to send out a healing thought; the consciousness of God-Presence becomes vivid. It illumines all until it reveals the perfect body. In other words, consciousness reveals life and health until it sees the true state of the patient; when this consciousness of Wholeness includes the patient we get the best healing. There is a spiritual uplift, an awakening of the consciousness of the one who desires to be healed, such as no other way of doing the work can accomplish.

I ask you to keep this in thought, because all of the healing that is done today is on one of these three planes. I do not condemn any one of these, but I advise you to remember always the highest, and work for that. Anyone can cure or heal, if he puts himself in the right mental attitude. He can do surface work through his will power, and the right kind of healing by putting his thought in the right relation to God.

A GROUP OF QUESTIONS

There are two ways in which to answer questions; one is from principle, and the other is from experience. Let me explain what I mean. People have come to me at different times saying, "Do you think such and such a thing can be healed? My answer according to Principle is, "Yes, I know that it can." "Have you seen it done?" is the question that often follows. When we answer simply from what we have seen, our answer accords with experience. When we answer from what we know can be done, our answer accords with Principle. Both are good; both are helpful. But do not base your acceptance of what can be done with this Truth by what you have seen or by what some one else has seen.

There would be no progress in the world, if we did not see beyond experience.

Marconi knew before he could send a message that such a thing was possible, and then he carried it out into experience. So it is with you and me; if we apply Principle, the Principle that lies back of everything the One Presence and the One Power, we shall know what can be done, whether it has been done or not.

If Jesus had waited to know what others had done before he attempted to live this way, the life of power would never have been lived by him. He was bold enough to see Truth ahead of what anyone had ever seen before, and he was brave enough to stand and live the truth he saw, alone. This is why he was so mighty, and why he demonstrated. Accordingly, do not let us ask, "Can this be done? Have you seen it?"

Let us learn Principle, and know for ourselves that "All things are possible to them that believe."

"Can every disease be healed?" This is answered above. If we go to Principle every time, we shall answer these questions within ourselves. Thousands and thousands are healed right along who have been pronounced incurable, not by one physician but by many. Sometimes a seeker will say, "Well, you know, this is one of the hardest things to heal, and I have never known a case like it to be healed." Some one says, "I have seen everything cured but deafness." Deafness has been healed; even if it had not been, there would be no reason for saying that it could not be; for whatever we see in Principle, we may declare boldly, "It can be done."

The power of our healing and the power of our living depends upon our attitude.

We must not listen to experience as a proof, but we must see the possibility from the standpoint of Principle. Every disease there is may be healed; I have seen every kind healed.

Are people receptive to healing whether or not they ask for it?

Yes. But there is a difference in people. Some do not ask for treatment because they do not know what it is; they are, however, in their souls, longing for truth, and whether or not they ask for it, they are ready to be helped. Of course, one who shuts himself off and is not receptive within can not be reached; or, if he is reached, it is by a long process of what would be very laborious work. There are so many ready to be helped that it is better to spend time with the many who are ready than to work with the one who is resisting.

What words shall we use when giving a treatment?

Do not think the word you use is all-important. Remember the word is a means to an end. Remember, also, another thing; a formula is a good thing in the beginning, but if adhered to too strictly, growth in understanding is retarded. Any formula is soon outgrown. It is well to give a patient some statement, some simple words of truth, to keep his thought on something besides his ills.

Let us not say that we will have no formulas, or that we must always have formulas. The highest and best healing is the consciousness·that goes forth without spoken words; but at times it is necessary to use the word; do not fear to do so. I feel so sure that the universal Spirit knows exactly what each one of us needs that, when I treat anyone, I sit at first perfectly quiet and receptive, thinking of God's Presence. I have the greatest faith that just exactly what is needed to be realized will be given; the right words, if words must be spoken. We can not make definite rules along that line.

As to how often the treatments should be given, that, the healer must decide; but bear this rule in mind, that the fewer treatments one can give to accomplish the work, the better.

Try to live so well, to be so conscious of the presence and the power of God that you need give but one treatment.

Give each treatment as though it were the only one, and give it with such consciousness that it will be the only one needed, if the patient is receptive. If there are more needed, give them until the patient realizes and manifests his wholeness.

Shall we treat those surrounding the patient?

We were taught at first to treat each member of the family, but it is being proved over and over again that we do not have to treat in that way. We can treat the little baby alone if our consciousness is clear and strong and we do not give power in our own thoughts to adverse conditions, as we call them; the one who believes in evil most is the one who is going to do the most treating.

When we see nothing but the presence and power of God, we shall know it includes all, and we shall trust it wholly.

Do Divine Scientists believe in medicine?

Principle, understood, will assure us there is no need for medicine. I have heard it said we often recommend both treatment and medicine.

Never is a physician recommended, never is medicine recommended by the one who sees Principle clearly.

Occasionally some one says to me, "I have been ill for two or three weeks and I had a physician; my husband (or my mother) insisted." I find that where there is just a little hankering for a physician there will generally be two or three outside who will say you should have one. I have found also that, to those who stand firm in the consciousness of the one Presence and Power, the husbands have not usually suggested a physician or any remedies. Divine Science does not recommend medicine. However, we do not condemn.

The one who understands the Divine Presence will never feel a need of anything else.

The question is asked, "Is it not helpful to have a diagnosis?"

It simply gauges the attitude of the healer at the time she recommends a diagnosis; she believes the disease is there, a something that she must call by name; she gives a reality to the claim.

The one who is positively conscious of God's presence and God's power, cares not for the name of the disease.

He realizes that the power of God is much more powerful than any name under heaven, and there is no temptation to learn human opinion.

What we need more than anything else, what the world needs, is those who are willing to stand for principle despite all that threatens. Do we think that something hard will come to us if we stand by principle? It can not be half so serious as the fact that we have swerved from principle.

Man's development is the supreme thing in the universe, and whatever tempts us to fall below the highest we see is withdrawing us from the fullest development to which our souls can come at that time. True to principle, no evil can possibly befall; I care not what the results may seem.

What is the true nature of the body?

It is most important for us to know the truth about the body for, thereby and by that alone, shall we free it from the many ills to which we have believed it heir.

To get the true perception of anything invisible or visible, we must continually refer to our Basis.

To learn the truth of the body, let us go to first principles of our teaching to find what is revealed to us there of the true nature of the body. Our fundamental statements are: God is Omnipresent; therefore, what God is, is omnipresent. God is Life, God is Mind, God is Spirit.

The God-Life, God-Mind, God-Substance is everywhere present; there is no other life, no other intelligence.

"I am and beside me there is none else, saith the Lord." "Of Him and through Him, and to Him are all things."

The Substance of the body is Spirit; there is nothing else for it to be. "That which is born of spirit is Spirit." "Like produces like." Knowing the body to be Spirit, we come into the perception of its true nature. We no longer condemn it to weakness and limitation. We see it as holy, as whole—an expression of Universal Life. We reap the fruits of our thoughts; for we begin to see the true state of the body.

The true state of the body is health.

XII

HOW CAN WE LIVE IN HARMONY
WITH OUR FELLOW BEINGS?

Purpose: To give the three Principles by the application of which harmonious relationships may be maintained with all.

Those who are living the new life should do more than "live peaceably with all men."

There should be a joyful harmony with all humanity, with all nature, with every living creature.

This is the new ideal and realization of it will reveal the new heaven and the new earth. "Thou shalt be in league with the stones of the field and the beasts of the field shall be at peace with thee," is a prophecy that is being understood today.

In this lesson we shall consider the problem of human relationship alone.

There are certain principles to be maintained in every relationship.

Supreme among these is the principle of integrity.

If there be a discordant element in the environment, let each person examine himself in some such way as this: Am I true in every detail of my relationship with this one, just as true as I should wish another to be to me? Do I think of him as I would desire him to think of me? Are my acts an evidence of integrity? Then again, let me ask myself: Am I giving this one his freedom just as I wish mine?

Loosing another, and letting him go as his guidance leads him is another essential of true relationship.

The holding of one's opinion over another or the condemnation of the action of another, although it may be unspoken, is the reason of much unhappiness between those who should rejoice in each other. The critical attitude toward a weaker one is often a cruel bondage to him.

Do I love this one? This is the third important question to be asked.

Love, remember, is that deep inner relation of unity which is evidenced as outstreaming good will.

When I love another, I feel at one with him, and this at-one-ment shows itself as true interest in his experiences, achievement, and growth; and as forgiveness, when he offends; also as a wish to be helpful in so far as his desire, and circumstances permit. It shows itself in prayer for him and faith in him; it is evidenced by keeping hands off when it is best that this should be.

We are not here to live for another; we are here to live our own lives to the best.

Our help to the world is through our own living.

To be joyful, loving, helpful, is our privilege, and herein lies our power. The most ineffective and undesirable person in the world is the sanctimonius egotist who goes about showing his fellow men how to be good.

There are two sides to every relationship, the outer and the inner. On the one hand, the encouraging word, the kind act; on the other— without this the outer is of but little value—

there is the inner tie, the *feeling of unity*. In this feeling of unity evidenced in outward cooperation, lies the power and harmony of every relationship.

Treat your every relationship by the practice of the three principles given—integrity, freedom, love— and you will prove their working power.

SOME PROBLEMS OF HOME LIFE

Many are puzzled to know how to solve the problems of daily life in the home. Various questions have been handed me concerning the conditions of poverty, overwork, and the disagreement of the family upon religious views.

Problems are settled from principle, not from experience.

There is a principle to guide the home life as there is a principle to guide our judgment in all things. When our conclusions are made from an unchanging principle, we shall see conditions and experiences conforming to that knowledge. To judge from changeable experiences is to have no certain knowledge. "Judge not by appearances," said Jesus. Experiences have their place, and will always exist for every action must have its results. The fruit of action is experience, and to interpret correctly, one must understand Principle.

Home life is most important because from it goes forth an influence upon every phase of life, business, religious, and social. The home influence should be the impetus to all the affairs of daily living. In the home we show what we really believe; in the outer world we may assume. At home we like to relax and are likely to think it unnecessary to be courteous, or we become careless of appearance and unguarded in our speech. Do not make home merely a place for eating and sleeping, or a place to go when there is nowhere else to go. We should find in our homes the heart-love and soul-culture that stimulates us to bring forth our best.

A home that is exclusive is not ideal.

Any individual who lives for himself alone never lays hold of the fullness of life—never fully lives.

While the home is the center of living and of action for its immediate members, yet its influence must extend far beyond its doors. Home is the individualized center. I love to compare the individual to the sun, a center of life.

The life of God should radiate from each of us.

Love is to be sent forth brightening all upon whom it falls, cheering whoever comes for a moment within its touch.

All can accept the ideal; but how can it be made practical?

First—Perfect Equality. This does not mean that each one is the master of the house, nor each the handmaid, but that each in his position is of equal importance. Is the hand above the foot or the hearing more necessary than the seeing? We need every member; the foot is as essential to the body as the hand.

Acknowledge the principle of equality in the home —one Mind, as the intelligence of all.

Accept all within your gates in the Truth of their Being, whether they are manifesting it or not.

Second—Co-operation. Each giving the best he has. It is as important to receive as to give; love equally to do both. Co-operation means working together for one end.

Third—Grant Liberty. Do not insist that others shall see as you see. As we demand, we must give. There may have been a time when we would have forced; but faith in the power of God makes us non-resistant. The more faith we have, the more liberty we give.

Liberty consists not only in keeping hands off but also in keeping thoughts off.

If we really believe that the Spirit of God is in each one, we can help another most by seeing that God is working in his life, and by trusting that God-power to lead him rightly. I know a home in which four religious faiths are represented, but the members of the family agree on religious freedom and there is not the least inharmony there.

XIII

CAN I CHANGE MY DISPOSITION?

Purpose: To give the one great rule by which we may overcome undesirable traits of temperament.

Those who are ignorant of the great principles of the Universe make many mistakes, and these mistakes bring peculiar and hard conditions into their environment. The promise is that we shall know the Truth and through this knowledge shall be freed. As soon as fundamental principles are perceived, our thoughts and actions change to accord with the new perception.

This laying hold of Truth, and embodying it in the day's experience is called living the new life.

It is a life new to us, when it is first attempted, but surely it is the kind of living that must be the Divine Intent for us.

However, into this Eden of new perception, new endeavor, and new realization of good, there sometimes slips the serpent of discord; and we wonder why, for we have supposed the day of problems to be over. While strides of progress are rapid in the early stages of the new life, we do not slough off at once the old habits of thought. Then, too, we are surrounded by suggestions of former conditions, and these make a strong appeal to us owing to our former firmly fixed beliefs. Therefore, even after our vision of Truth is quite clear, there is still work ahead of us, the work of outgrowing the deeply rooted undesirable habits of thought and feeling.

— 64 —

There are many who have attained heights of spirituality in certain directions whose power and usefulness are greatly limited by temperament, infixed wrong habits of thought and feeling. If in the old way they were domineering, they may carry this habit into the new as dictatorialness and intolerance of others' views. The old ambition to get ahead may now seem to them spiritual aspiration. Selfishness may be called by them, evolving ego. Self-indulgence, sensitiveness, and other traits may be translated into the new thought regime and prevent one's attaining his highest.

Fortunately, Divine Science gives us a standard up to which we must measure. Jesus had this high ideal and gave it to us:"Be ye perfect even as your Father in heaven is perfect." This is lofty aspiration, and yet there can be nothing below it for us. If we wish to perfect ourselves in any line of human activity, we know that we must study and work. We must learn the principles that govern our work, and be true to these in practice. There is no achievement without this.

So it is with spiritual development; we must understand the principles of life, and practice these principles in our daily living.

There should be no discouragement to us in this high ideal and the necessity for earnest endeavor that it entails.

We have within us and around us the great Presence, loving us, stimulating us, helping us with Its wonderful Power.

Then, too, the joy of attaining is so great; as great perhaps as attainment itself, and no one who is steadfast in endeavor can fail.

In our work for overcoming undesirable traits of disposition there is one splendid rule that helps us perceive rightly and rectify quickly any mistakes we are making. The rule is this: To make it our practice when a thought or feeling surges through us to ask the question, "Would God think this thought; would God feel this way?"

If our thought or feeling could not be entertained by the Mind of Infinite Wisdom and Love, it does not belong to us, for in our true nature we are Godlike.

This is the simplest and most effective rule I know. Practiced persistently and serenely it opens one's vision to his mental mistakes and brings to him the realization of his God-Being. This is joy ineffable. In this realization is soul satisfaction.

XIV

WHAT IS OUR HEREDITY?

These are answers to letters received by Miss Brooks, and are placel here because they deal with a vital subject.

My dear Mary,

God is your Father and you inherit His own Substance. His perfect activity is working in you always. When you realize this you will experience health.

You say, "The Bible teaches the inheritance of disease." Remember the threat in the second commandment is "to them that hate me." You are too enlightened to hate. The answer to this commandment is found in the eighteenth chapter of Ezekiel. Listen to these words:

"Yet say ye, Why? doth not the son bear the iniquity of the Father? When the son hath done that which is lawful and right, and hath kept all my statutes, and hath done them, he shall surely live.

"The soul that sinneth, it shall die. The son shall not bear the iniquity of the father neither shall the father bear the iniquity of the son: the righteousness of the righteous shall be upon him, and the wickedness of the wicked shall be upon him.

"But if the wicked will turn from all his sins that he hath committed, and keep all my statutes and do that which is lawful and right, he shall surely live, he shall not die.

"All his transgressions that he hath committed, they shall not be mentioned unto him: in his righteousness that he hath done he shall live.

"Have I any pleasure at all that the wicked should die? saith the Lord God: and not that he should return from his ways, and live?"

Again you say, "We see about us many cases of inherited disease." True, but we must recognize the fact that what we see is the result of belief in human heredity.

When we refuse to believe anything but Divine Inheritance, we shall demonstrate perfect health.

Physical laws do not teach inheritance of disease. It has been demonstrated beyond a doubt that disease is never transmitted to offspring. The fact that parents believe in the possibility of such transmission conveys to the child a tendency in that direction. If the child can be taken into an entirely different environment and surrounded by an atmosphere of trust, the tendency is nullified.

As to your being "a demonstration of it," this demonstration is but evidence of race belief. When you realize that you are a manifestation of God, and that His Life, Love, Wisdom, and Power work in and through you, you will demonstrate and enjoy the blessing of perfect health.

May you soon come to this realization.

———

My dear Tom,

You say that God permits disease even if He does not send it.

The truth is that God knows nothing about disease.

The Bible does not teach physical inheritance, although it seems to teach many things that could not be true of a God of Love.

On the other hand we find there statements that declare us to be sons of God; that enjoin us to be perfect even as our Father in heaven is perfect; that assert perfect freedom for us through knowledge of Truth.

The lesser teaching must give place to the greater. Let us read our Bibles, keeping ever in thought the omnipresence of a God of Love. Then shall we get the true understanding of this wonderful book.

We read, "If thine eye be single thy whole body shall be full of light." When the eye is single to the light of God's Love, there can be no conception of germs to tear down and to devour as you believe them to be doing in your case.

You say that you overworked, thus violating a natural law, and that you are suffering for this now. There is a higher law than the so-called natural law. Your activity is from God and your strength in Him is limitless. "Ye shall mount up on wings, as eagles, ye shall run and not be weary."—From Isaiah 40:31.

You receive Life directly from God. He thinks you, creates you, perfect like Himself. He is living you now and sees you only as He creates you, pure and perfect. You inherit from God only that which is good—His Wisdom, Love, Health, Power, and Joy. In this perception of Truth is your salvation from every ill.

Will you not accept this truth about yourself? If you would only cease resisting!

"Nearer is He than breathing,
Closer than hands or feet."

Talk to this loving Presence. Work your tiny bit of faith, and make it grow.

XV

WHAT IS THE GREATEST HUMAN ACHIEVEMENT?

Purpose: To emphasize this Truth: That to know God's will and to fulfill His purpose in our lives is the greatest human achievement.

In one sense there is no human achievement, for whatever we accomplish is wrought by the power of Divine Wisdom and Love inherent within us. God works by means of man, and every achievement is the outcome of this Presence and Power. The greatest human achievement is not to be found in externals, not in the building of cities, nor in the execution of great commercial schemes, not even in our wonderful works of art.

Our highest attainment comes through the inner revelation; it is to learn God's Plan and to realize this Divine Purpose within ourselves.

In order to fulfill our destiny, we must know God as the Omnipresent One, whose nature is goodness, love, life, power. We must come into the realization of our oneness with the Father; we must see that we are destined to become the companion of the Infinite; we must attain unto the measure of the stature of Christ.

That to which we give attention becomes magnified in our mentality.

If our thought is centered upon disease, lack, sorrow, our mental sun will cease to shine, and the world will be very dark to us. On the other hand, when we refuse to entertain these hobgoblins and persistently give ourselves to the Truth of God-Presence with its infinite Goodness, the great light of Love, Joy, and Peace, breaks within us, and problems are no more. They cannot stand in the light of Truth.

In order to outgrow problems, we must have faith in the laws of Life; God wishes us to know the Truth, wishes us to be free. What we call law is but God's method of bringing about his own purposes. Therefore, the laws of Life are working to bring to us the knowledge that is our freedom. Faith in law means that we do not resist the processes of our unfoldment, but trust the law absolutely, because we know that it is bringing us to the realization of our good. Our growth will be entirely harmonious when we have this perfect trust. It is resistance, through lack of faith in the working of the law, that makes conditions hard.

The non-resistant attitude that comes from faith in the working of the law, is powerful to dissolve every inharmonious condition.

One of the breeders of problems is our absorption in the getting of things.

We should abound in all good things; but we shall realize this abundant supply of health, and of all else, only when our supreme purpose is Truth and Righteousness.

All good is now ours, but we must realize it through spiritual consciousness. When we seek earnestly the best gifts, when our thought is aglow with aspiration for the highest, what we call the problems of the day do not disturb us.

We pass no opinion upon these, but use them as stepping-stones to greater realization. If we are faithful in the practice of self-training in the great spiritual principles of living until the old habits of unbelief fall away, we receive the crown of life—perfect realization. In the new blessedness that comes to us, there is no darkness, no shadow of night, for lo, all things have become new.

God's will must be Godlike.

We cannot conceive of God willing for us sickness or sorrow, weakness or sin. We have come to know that these inharmonies are the result of man's ignorance. As he is enlightened by Truth they will disappear. God wills for us only life, health, goodness, love, and power. He wills that we should be wise in our day's decisions. He wills that we should be loving, kind, uncritical, fearless, trustful, joyful. He wills brotherhood throughout the land; and, also that we should say with Jesus and Paul, "I of myself do nothing, the Father in me doeth the works." If we understand God's will in this way, and try steadfastly to fulfill it, we find ourselves gradually freed from bondage to race hypnotism. Self-centered thought—selfishness--goes. We forgive perfectly. We serve efficiently. From our earnest endeavor comes clear vision. We are led definitely not only to understand the great principles of right living but also to know God's immediate intent for us. We know whether God wishes us to go forth or to be still, to give or to withhold, to cherish or to lose. Such is the life of power.

This is the greatest human achievement, this knowing the God-Will and fulfilling the Divine Purpose.

Let me make a suggestion to all of those who earnestly desire this great achievement. Since Jesus is the one who has attained beyond all others, let us study his life, not merely to get the historical setting or to be able to picture his personality and environment, but in order to lay hold of the knowledge that was his, the motive that impelled, the love that radiated through him.

Jesus was conscious of God; so must we be. Jesus knew his own relation to God, "I and my Father are one"; so must we know our oneness with the Father. Jesus so lived and so loved, that his very presence was a healing power. So must we live and love, if we, like Jesus, are to bear witness unto the Truth, and thus attain to the great achievement.

XVI

WHAT IS REAL AND WHAT IS ILLUSION?

Purpose: To lead the student to deep insight into, and true evaluation of the world about him; that he may delight in it as only the spiritually discerning can.

Man in all ages and in every stage of his development has sought Something higher than himself, and seeking, has found. "Man is incurably religious." Civilized men have simply continued the search begun by primitive men ages ago. Both have found; each in his own way.

It is essential that men hold the right belief about God, for the history of man accords with his belief in God; our weakness or our strength as world citizens is determined thereby.

The following statements are true: As man is, so is his God; as is man's conception of God, so is man. Man conceives God according to his own development; and his conception reacts upon him as an individual. Until he becomes enlightened, man conceives God to be manlike; the conception of a tyrannical God sprang from tyrants, and has brought tragic experiences into the world—persecution, the inquisition, and mental cruelty. The conception of a loving God, as taught by Jesus, is transforming men's lives; it is impelling them to translate the theory of human brotherhood into daily practice.

The need through the ages has been a concept of God that will bring out the nearness—the oneness of God and Man; the Divine Science idea of God as Infinite and Immediate Presence, does this for me.

In Divine Science we think of God as the Infinite Expanse of Consciousness—the Fundamental Being of the Universe; but we also know God as infinitely loving Presence "closer than breathing, nearer than hands or feet"—the very Essence of our Being, the LIFE that you and I are.

There are myriads of ways in which this Life expresses, from the grain of sand to the solar system, from the wayside flower to man, but *all* is one Life. God Life is expressing Itself as creation. God is sharing His Life with us, his children; He is truly in us, through us, around us. Man is always being lived by God; the Father of us all is not only the far, He is the near; the Fatherhood of God is both infinite and immediate.

The truth that God lives in each one of us makes the individual potentially infinite.

There is no limit to what he can comprehend and to what he can do, as he comes to realize his oneness with the Father. It is not of ourselves, remember, that we are powerful; it is of the Father which dwelleth in us and worketh through us. The life of the individual is endless, and each one of us will go on throughout eternity, realizing more and more the truth of God-Life.

Truth is changeless, but our conceptions change; these grow deeper and broader and truer as we unfold.

The Law of God is eternal, and our interpretation of the Law deepens and broadens and becomes truer as we develop.

Let us suppose that Jesus had said, "I see a new interpretation of law, but what Moses said must not be changed; we must live by the old." Think of the loss to humanity such a conception would have meant. Jesus taught, on the contrary, that the Spirit of Truth would lead men into greater and greater knowledge. "When he, the Spirit of Truth, is come, he will guide you into *all* truth."

Led by the Spirit of Truth we are finding the fundamental things of life, and the welfare of man is being assured by this deepening, enlarging, and strengthening of his concept of God.

We are coming to see that the universe of form is the manifestation of Infinite Consciousness and that the intelligence of God is everywhere in the universe.

God Idea is taking form. What shall we do with the inharmony that we see around us? Does God create deformity, sin, and suffering? At this point let us take up the question as to what is real and what illusion.

Each philosophy has its own vocabulary. To some the real means the actual, the objective only. This concept leaves out the part of the Universe that is most important. There are others to whom the real means the subjective wholly; to them outer force, outer action, and form are not real. Here again a part of the Universe is denied.

The one who thinks of the actual in the sense of what he can see, hear, and touch, and calls this the only real is dealing with the outer merely, and is accepting the doctrine of materialism. The one who believes that only the invisible or subjective is real excludes an important part of the universe. The materialist is looking at the external only; if he were willing to look through the external, he would find God and God in action.

The real is more than that which is becoming or coming forth; it is more than that which is visible or than that which is invisible. Let us hold the bigger attitude. Why try to wipe out the visible or refuse to accept the invisible? God is all. Truth is eternal. Because we do not see the whole of Truth, let us not deny the part. Human ignorance cannot do away with the visible, for the visible is God in expression, but it is a mistake to believe in the visible alone.

The Universe is one—visible and invisible.

Divine Science gives the truest interpretation of the Universe that I have found.

Again we are told that, "*What is,* is real." But I ask, "Do we really know *what is?*" The senses do not report aright. They do not tell us *what is.* As we stand on the back platform of a rapidly moving train our eyes report that the rails are coming together behind us. Is this true? The senses report that the sun rises in the east every morning and sets in the west at evening. For thousands of years men believed that the earth was flat, because it looked that way to the eye. As we look over the plains our eyes show us that the earth and the sky meet; while natural science proves that there is limitless space above and around us.

We have all heard people say, "I know this is true because I have seen it." Is seeing believing? It is not, according to the latest theories advanced by natural scientists. You and I look at a piece of furniture—a chair or a table. Do we see it as it is? What appears to us as solid substance, firm and hard, is *really* atoms, vivid with life activity, vibrating in unison with one another.

There is no inanimate matter.

Natural science tells us that the only difference between various kinds of material, such as air or wood or steel, lies in the number of electrons that revolve around each of the nuclei that make up the material. We do not become aware of this pulsating life activity through the report of the senses.

Is seeing, believing? I say that I went down town today and bought blue material for a dress. Really the material I bought is blue because it isn't blue; the color that you and I see is what we call blue because the material does not absorb certain rays and does absorb others. That which it rejects and reflects gives the material its blue color. It is evident that we cannot rely upon the senses.

Are you saying, "I learn by experience?" Is this true? Are our experiences always based upon Truth? What shall we trust since we have found that the report of the senses is not dependable? The subconscious? No, we cannot trust it, for the subconscious accepts without question what is said to it by the senses, until it is trained by the right thinking of the individual to higher standards. The subconscious inherits much ignorance, and it believes in sin, sickness, and death until you and I teach it better. Since

the subconscious may report negatively, we dare
not rely upon its promptings. Generations have
done this; mankind has gathered its records of
the past in this way. As a consequence, many
times we are working from the wrong basis.
The subconsious tries to report to us that we
are creatures of a dire heredity, bound by past
mistakes and wrong beliefs.

**We are, in Truth, sons of God, free to progress
eternally.**

God, we affirm, is the one Reality of the
Universe. "What," I hear someone say, "I
have understood that Divine Science believed in
nature, the created world. Now you are denying it." And I reply, "No, I am not denying the
universe of form and force; these are Immanuel,
God with us."

Here comes an exceedingly vital point:

**Perceiving Omnipresence clearly brings the realiza-
tion of health, supply, abundance, power, and joy.**

Before man does anything, the idea is in his
mind. For example, the architect has the plan
in mind before attempting to build; the real
cathedral is in mind. An engineer works out his
plans for construction in his thought before he
builds. A dressmaker has the plan of the dress
worked out mentally before she cuts the
material. So it is with God!

**Every created thing is Idea in Divine Mind before
it is expressed.**

One of the unchanging laws of the Universe is
that, like produces like. Jesus stated this law in
these words: "Do men gather grapes of thorns
or figs of thistles?"

"Even so every good tree bringeth forth good fruit; but a corrupt tree bringeth forth evil fruit."

We are not surprised, since like produces like, that God looked upon the works of His creation and pronounced these good. Yes, very good! They were Godlike! God is looking upon His works today, and He is pronouncing them good. Blessed is the man who discerning Reality—God-Presence—pronounces all Good.

Are we prepared in the light of what has been said, to define the Real? Divine Science says that the Real is That Which Eternally Is—God and God in action. This means Mind and its Ideas, the principles and laws of the Universe, and That Which God Does.

What God Is and What God Does Is the Real.

What man conceives apart from God or in belief of separation from God is the outcome of ignorance and does not accord with God-Idea, nor with Universal Principle; hence it is the unreal or illusion.

Glenn Clark in *The Soul's Sincere Desire*, discriminates between the real and the unreal in the following words: "Reality, in the eyes of the practical man, is made up of cold, hard facts. And what are the cold, hard facts of life? As we look about us in this world, what we see all too frequently are quarrels, bickerings, unhappiness, unfaithfulness, treachery, covetousness and materialism everywhere. These are the facts of life. Fact comes from the word, *factum,* meaning something that *we* do or make. Are these facts of life identical with the realities of life? Not according to Jesus.

To him Reality does not consist of that which is made, but of that which eternally is.

Love is—quarrels are made; *joy is*—unhappiness is made; *truth is*—lies are made; *loyalty is*—betrayals are made; *purity is*—impurity is made; *life is*—sickness is made.

Is nature real according to our definition of Reality? Let us look at a flower; richness of color, beauty of form, and sweetness of fragrance are there. The flower is real because it conforms to the fundamental conception of its Being, the God-Idea of it, although temporarily expressed. The idea of the flower in God-Mind is eternal and real; and its expression is temporal and real.

All expression, true to Idea and Principle, whether coming directly from God or from God through man, is real.

You say that the sunset is temporal; its glory is passing: Is it any the less beautiful for this reason? The sunset in all its colorful glory passes, but the Idea of the sunset is eternal. The principle upon which it is based and by which it is expressed is Real, the permanent Real, while the sunset itself is the temporary real.

How rich, wonderful, and beautiful Creation is! Some philosophers say "amen" to all that I have said—One God Omnipresent; One Creator, God; One Creation, Godlike, hence perfect; and in the next breath, perhaps, they speak of man's creation. Here is a strange teaching. We do not agree with it. This is where Divine Science stands true to its basic principle.

When we speak the word, Omnipresence, we mean that One and One only is the Reality.

Illusion is believing in more than one—the many; it teaches an opposite to the One wholly good—the devil or evil. Divine Science recognizes One Creator and only One, and this Creator is God.

We believe that unillumined thinking is the only evil in the universe.

Since God is Omnipresent, Life, Health, Beauty, Power, Intelligence and Joy are Omnipresent. Belief in aught else is delusion. From the point of view of Omnipresence we can say, "Whatever is, is Real."

There is only God and God in action.

Our conception that there is an opposite of God-Life, of harmony, and of good, is substanceless and has in it no power. Such misconceptions as that of the existence of two powers, one good and one evil, keep us from realizing the blessings of the Kingdom of God within us, of the Kingdom of Heaven at hand. As long as man is ignorant of Reality he will suffer the pangs of delusion—sin, sickness, and death.

We must know the Truth about Life. Jesus says, "Ye shall know the truth and the truth shall make you free."

Knowledge of God gives us understanding of Reality; in the light of God-Consciousness all illusion falls away, and through the practice of the Presence of God in thought, word, and deed, we come to know with unswerving certainty that there is only One Reality—God and God in action.

XVII

WHEN SHALL WE REALIZE OUR GOOD?

Purpose: To urge the student to withdraw his thought from over much dwelling in the past or on the future that he may give special attention to the richness and beauty of the present.

Now is the day of salvation.—II Cor. 6:2.

Come, for all things are now ready.—Luke 14:17.

There is an old habit of thought that still clings to us; the yielding to which retards us in our spiritual development. By "us," I mean those who have decided that the thing of most importance to the individual, the one thing needful, is knowledge of Truth. For we know that consciousness of Truth will bring the realization of that perfect harmony for which the soul of each one longs.

Have you noticed how little our thoughts dwell in the present? They are continually reverting to the past or turning to the future. This is the habit to which I refer. The present moment with all its fullness is, by many, given but little consideration compared to the thought given to the past and future. This habit of thought is a mistake. By lingering in the past we let ourselves be bound by the events and experiences that we call therefrom. Think well over this, for it means far more than can be seen at first glance.

We also make a mistake when we let our thoughts dwell in the future, for this gets us into the habit of postponement; or should I reverse this and say that, because we do not understand the fulness of the present, we postpone, we look to the future for our good; therefore, our thoughts turn naturally to where we believe our treasure to be.

The truth is that if we make it our chief aim to sound the depth of the present, we shall find it so full of riches, so altogether satisfying that there will be no chance for longing, no room for emptiness. The soul will become so filled with the consciousness of good that it will exclaim, "My cup runneth over!" "For he satisfieth the longing soul, and filleth the hungry soul with goodness." Now is always the important moment.

All that is interesting, vital, and true is concentrated in the present hour.

And, yet, we crucify the consciousness of the present between recollection of the past and anticipation of the future. When the thief on the cross, looking for his good as something to come, said "Lord, remember me when thou comest into thy Kingdom," Jesus' answer was, "Verily, I say unto thee, *Today* shalt thou be with me in paradise."

Jesus said unto Martha, "Thy brother shall rise again."

Martha saith unto him, "I know that he shall rise again in the resurrection at the last day."

Jesus said unto her, "*I am* the resurrection and the life."

It was this consciousness of ever-present Life with all that it means that enabled Jesus to speak the word with such authority that life and health and supply were immediately manifest.

Let us get an understanding of the present and live today, solely and wholly for today. This is the only way to find the living God.

"God himself is the Perpetual Now." When he gave his name to Moses, he said, "I Am That I Am." Only when we live in the present do we commune with Him, the ever-present God, the eternal Now.

"We do not enter immortality by thinking of a future life, but by communing with God and infinite realities now."

"He only knows the future well who knows the present well. The wise man can forsee, because he can see. Insight is the only foresight."

And, again it has been said, "We escape a future hell by coming out of our present hells. We reach a future heaven by the portal of a present heaven."

Two-thirds of the happy life of a child is due to the fact that it is so much absorbed in the present. Its little mishaps are not aggravated by the remembrance of past evil or by the fear of evil to come, nor are its joys lessened thereby. It does not brood over past sorrows nor long for future good; it is joyous in present possession.

"But," you may ask, "is it not necessary, in order to shape our lives aright, to remember past experiences that we may get the lessons they teach and plan wisely for the future?"

When, with all earnestness, we turn our attention to the present and search for its riches, we find here with us always a Teacher far above the accumulated experiences of the entire world.

We find here equipment for the whole of life, present and future, and for every conceivable condition of life. We do not have to go to the past or to the future for anything. We do not have to search outside ourselves for any good we seek; "The kingdom of God is within you." "Seek ye first the kingdom of God and his righteousness and all these things shall be added unto you."

Jesus laid even greater stress on the doctrine of the Eternal Now.

This consciousness of the fullness of the present was the secret of Jesus' power.

And it may be the foundation of power in you and me, in each one who says, "Now is the time for the fulfillment of all things." The Father was in no wise more generous to Jesus than he is to us, but Jesus made better use of the gifts than we have; he kept himself free from every encumbrance; he did not permit the least weight of doubt, fear, ignorance or sin to rest upon him He was free and open to the whole Truth, an unobstructed channel for the outshining of every divine attribute.

The Holy Spirit that came upon the disciples as they tarried at Jerusalem was nothing more or less than the coming to them of the consciousness of the perfect Now, the fullness of the present. Filled with this consciousness, they went forth to their mighty works, and with this same realization, so may we.

Without this consciousness, we are nothing; with it, all things are possible unto us.

James Freeman Clarke says, "The Christian church has often backslidden to the standpoint of Brahmanism in asserting that heaven must be postponed to the next world, and that it is necessary to be miserable and sinful as long as we live in this one. It has loved to say that former days were better than these, and to complain of the degeneracy of the times. But true Christianity never does this. It looks at the Now as miraculous and full of a divine spirit. It makes the world full of God now—nature full of God, man a child of God, the Holy Spirit coming and dwelling in all hearts that open themselves to receive it.

"What we need, therefore, at this time as much as ever, is to believe in a present salvation, and to be sure that Now is the accepted time. We need a God at hand, not afar off; a present and not a past inspiration; a present Savior, a present immortality, an eternal life abiding in us and a heaven in our midst."

I wish we might lay aside all thought, all remembrance of the past, its events and experiences. I wish we might put from us the vision of the future with what seem to be its demands upon us, and enter fully into the Now by concentrating our attention wholly upon the present moment. For this is the only time that concerns us, the only time we need be careful of or watchful over; the future must become the present before we can live it. If we get from the Now all that is here for us, so full of all that is desirable will this consciousness become to us that it will run over on both sides, and we shall find the present including within itself the whole of the future and all of the past; for here and now is the fulness of eternity.

The past has gone from us, and the future never is, but is always going to be; therefore, the present is the only time that is truly ours, and it contains the whole of Truth and the Truth of the whole.

Close the eyes for a few moments and let the thought dwell upon the One Presence that we know is here, eternally filling heaven and earth —above all, through all and in all.

In doing this, we find, first of all, the consciousness of peace. This must come when we recognize nothing but the One Presence. All conflict, every inharmonious condition of whatever nature or however real it may seem to us, is but the result of our yielding to the belief of two powers, one good and one evil, that will continue to war against each other until one or the other is destroyed. While we may feel that good will finally triumph, the present conflict presses hard upon us; therefore, this consciousness of peace is welcome and restful and very precious to us, for it prepares the soul for a fuller revelation of Truth.

I hesitate before this higher vision, for who can describe it—and who can receive it? Only he that dwelleth in the secret place of the Most High.

In this vision, we see God only and God as All in all, whose Presence bright fills all; whose Life is the life of all; whose Love is the nature of the whole; whose Substance, eternal and changeless is manifested

in living forms as eternal and perfect as God Himself
is perfect.

What more can be said? Not much—but
infinitely more can be realized, for infinity itself
lies before us and eternity is ours—Now.

CPSIA information can be obtained at www.ICGtesting.com
Printed in the USA
LVOW04s1458250515

439803LV00018B/938/P